"Thank you Neisha for this very inspiring and thought-filled book. This is a book that I will share with all my friends who have daughters."

– BECKY CORTEZ

"*Shine* is a breath of fresh air, and a must-read book for moms! We live in a culture that has become obsessed with tip-toeing around important issues, so as to not "trigger" anyone. In her book, Neisha Hernandez gives us straight talk about stepping up and owning the responsibility we have to lead and teach our daughters. She expresses, in clear, direct language, the need for all of us to examine our priorities and lead by example. If you are looking for practical advice for raising strong girls in an increasingly confusing world, read this book!"

– DARCY FAGERWOLD
OWNER/DIRECTOR
EXPRESSIONS DANCE AND MOVEMENT CENTER

"*Shine* by Neisha Hernandez is a much-needed and highly accessible roadmap for parents to inspire and guide their daughters (and sons) to live a visionary life, to find and achieve their dreams, and to uplift others through example and service. *Shine* gives us simple and profound steps to discover and prioritize our most treasured core values. It gives easy-to-use examples which can be used daily to model, teach, and motivate our children to find their own inner compass, in their choice of media, friends, mentors, life work and service to others. Thank you Neisha for the gift of *Shine*."

– Anita H. Hickey, M.D.

Shine

Shine

A Mom's Guide to Help Her Daughter Find and Follow Her Dreams

Neisha Hernandez

NEW YORK

LONDON • NASHVILLE • MELBOURNE • VANCOUVER

Shine

A Mom's Guide to Help Her Daughter Find and Follow Her Dreams

© 2019 Neisha Hernandez

Published in New York, New York, by Morgan James Publishing in partnership with Difference Press. Morgan James is a trademark of Morgan James, LLC. www.MorganJamesPublishing.com

ISBN 9781642792836 paperback
ISBN 9781642792843 eBook
ISBN 9781642793161 audiobook
Library of Congress Control Number: 2018911286

Cover Design by:
Christopher Kirk
www.GFSstudio.com

Interior Design by:
Chris Treccani
www.3dogcreative.net

Morgan James is a proud partner of Habitat for Humanity Peninsula and Greater Williamsburg. Partners in building since 2006.

Get involved today! Visit
MorganJamesPublishing.com/giving-back

Dedication

For Riley, Sydney, Luke, and Stella –
May Your Light Shine Bright!

Table of Contents

Chapter 1
Supermom

"My mother is my root, my foundation. She planted the seed that I base my life on, and that is the belief that the ability to achieve starts in your mind."
— MICHAEL JORDAN

Meet Jennifer. More than anything else in life, Jennifer wants to raise her daughter Lily to be an extraordinary person who loves God and loves others, is healthy, has good character, morals, values, principles, and ethics. She wants Lily to be happy while making a contribution to society. And Lily, like most young girls, wants the world on a platter! More than anything else, Lily dreams of becoming a ballerina. Being a dedicated and dutiful working mother, Jennifer enrolls her daughter in dance lessons of all kinds. And through her years of faithful training, Lily begins to progress in her technique. She is growing in performance ability and shows great promise of becoming a professional dancer someday. Mom spends her afternoon hours at the dance school, supporting Lily in her efforts, volunteering at the school, and chatting it up with the other moms. Lily is displaying extraordinary results and Jennifer is proud beyond words.

The mommy talk in the lobby is always about the kids. Another mom boasts about how she has not been at dance with this child, because she has been at the basketball court five days a week with her other child. Another mom shares that she is juggling dance and soccer. On Saturday, of course, they will be gone all day with the travelling soccer team. And IF they win, they will be travelling on Sunday too. And still another talks about pulling her kids from dance because grades are suffering. Dance is the only thing her child loves and she hopes that by threatening to take dance away, the child will make improvements in school. In the meantime, they are going into debt on tutoring sessions five days a week. These moms agree that they are doing whatever it takes to help their children reach their potential.

But these moms have more in common than their willingness to support their kids. In the quiet confidence between good friends, Jennifer vulnerably shares with Marie, another mom, that social media seems to be swallowing Lily's free time. "Who are these strangers influencing my Lily?" And Marie shares through tears that she completely missed her daughter's class project because she was at work. Her coworker told her, "If you want to be promoted, you have to show that work is your priority." Marie felt paralyzed and trapped in the space between wanting to be present for her daughter and wanting to make a living to provide for her daughter. The women hug it out with kind words to one another but both walk away feeling Mommy Guilt.

Later on in the hallway, another mom shares with Jennifer that although she has had the credentials and expertise for the promotion from schoolteacher to Vice Principal or Principal for four years, she has not applied for the job because she wanted to keep her children her priority. Now that her daughters are older, she will be making the leap and submitting her application to the district. She confides that she still isn't sure if this is what she wants because her priority is with her girls. She wants more than anything to raise happy, thriving kids who know their purpose in life!

Despite how hard these moms try, they are worried that they will fail as a mom. It's the saddest thing and a big problem for us working moms. We seem to wrestle with the balance of parenting our daughters and careers. Time is rushing away and we desperately need that time to connect with our daughters. We are worried about outside influences in our daughters' world, and want to get life under control so we can help our girls grow into their gifts and really SHINE!

Jennifer is what I call a Supermom. She is an engaged mother, who also happens to work. She provides for her family, helps with homework, volunteers to chaperone and be room mother, and takes her daughter to her dance classes. But she wants more for her child. What about teaching Lily how to lead a balanced life, learning how to make correct choices (like when watching YouTube), and learning what her purpose in life is? How do you teach life purpose when you are busy at work and not able to balance life yourself? This life does not come with a GPS or a how-to manual and it's hard to work, get everyone taxied to where they need to go, do the household chores, AND help your daughter's dreams come true. But doing the last part well is Jennifer's goal. Seeing Lily reach her goal of becoming the ballerina that she dreams of becoming is Jennifer's dream come true.

I ask you, dear reader, do these Mama shares hit close to home? Do you feel empathy in your gut or your chest because you understand how it feels and don't know what to do either? If you take dance out of the story and replace it with whatever activity your child does – be it swimming, volleyball, or tennis – does the story sound familiar?

Your child has big dreams and you want to A) help her reach them and B) be there for it all. But with all of life's challenges, how do you do it? First, know you are not alone. I have lived this story and observed/commiserated with countless mommies living it over the last 30 years. We want more than coping mechanisms ... we want to be a GREAT parent and enjoy the process. Mom, you can help your daughter to live her dreams and have an amazing, impactful life! You will learn how your daughter can be the exception. Raise her to be a high-performance achiever!

Chapter 2
We Want the Same Thing

"Acceptance, tolerance, bravery, compassion.
These are the things my mom taught me."
— LADY GAGA

Moms, I am in the trenches with you. I own several businesses and have four kids. I know firsthand what a gift it is to be a mother. I also know the demands and the struggles. I try to be Supermom too. Have you ever heard the radio host Dr. Laura? It's her mission to protect kids, and part of that mission is encouraging moms to stay home instead of being at work when kids are home. Well, I believe her when she says it is best for children if Mom raises them. So, I strive to get all my work completed before my kids wake up in the morning and while they are at school so that I can be home and fully present with my children after school. (It is actually 4 a.m. right now as I write this book!) My goal is for my kids to think I am a stay at home mom. In fact, I just asked my six-year-old what she thought I did for work and she said, "I don't know ... sometimes you have meetings." Reality is, they know I work – they see me doing it sometimes. But, I put my children first and filter all my decisions through the lens of what is best for them. Like you, I want to help my children to grow into healthy, integrity-filled, happy, *super* versions of themselves. And like you, I understand Mommy Guilt because I have lived it. I searched for many, many years to try and solve the "Balance" problem. That's a whole other book itself, right? My point is, I have shared this journey and come through it. I can help you. I am going to let you off the hook right now with my big A-ha ... there is no such thing as balanced life. It does not exist. What there *is* instead is good planning and being fully present wherever you are. So that's my new goal. I have let the guilt go. I do the best I can when at work; I do the best I can when I am at home. I apply my signature SHINE system to every important area in my life and I hear the opera lady singing ... AHHHHHHHHH! I feel so much better.

For 30 years, I have taught ballet to children ages 18 months to 18 years. With the exception of being a mom, teaching ballet has been my greatest joy. When I look into a child's eyes and see that they "get" a concept, it's like a light turns on in their eyes and they are literally shining. That feeling warms my heart and I know beyond a shadow of a doubt that teaching is what I was born to do. We are all given gifts at birth and one of mine is sharing the gift of dance and music with children.

When I opened my first dance studio, my goal was to *make dancers*! But after a while I learned that less than one percent of any ballet class would ever go on to be professionals. If creating professional dancers was my goal, I was going to be spinning my wheels. One percent is not very much! So I dug deep to find a new "why." I loved dance – I have been all-consumed by it since the age of three. But why teach it? That's when I found my mentor, Misty Lown, who among many other great accomplishments founded *More than Just Great Dancing,* a Dance Studio Affiliate Program. After one day with her, I knew that although I would indeed continue to train some kids to go on to be professional dancers, my purpose was to encourage kids to lead inspired lives. The vehicle I would use to do the encouraging would be dance. I adopted Misty's vision – I would not be "teaching dance to make great dancers," I would be "teaching dance to make great kids." This has been my goal ever since and it is a deeply fulfilling mission. Just this week, a grandmother to one of my students pulled me aside to share her story. Her granddaughter recently had a near-death experience and the therapist asked the grandmother to find her a safe place in the world that she could mentally return to when she needed it. She chose the dance classroom. *This* is what propels me now. I hear the opera lady singing again.

At the time I am writing this book, my kiddos range from kindergarten to a senior in high school. Like I said, I try to make all important life decisions through the filter and lens of family first and I aim (and most days make it) to be home after school to be the minivan mom, running kids here and there. Family dinner is a requirement every day and I am the one to cook it. Like you, I too strive to be SUPERMOM. And like you, I too have my fair share of failures, self-disappointments, and Mommy Guilts. One Mom recently asked me with wide eyes, "You too? You miss the mark too?" OMG – YES! Being a mom has a WIDE and LONG learning curve.

When I was very young, as early as eight years old, my dad would play his cassette tapes in the car (I know! Cassette tapes – I am dating myself!!). Nine out of ten times, what came out of the car speaker was Earl Nightingale, Dennis Waitley, Zig Ziglar, and Wayne Dyer. If you have never heard of these greats, let me tell you what you are missing. These men, (may they all rest in peace), were the original inspirational speakers. They taught about mindset and work habits, pursuing a career that you love, how you become what you think about, and the power of positive thinking. Without realizing what was happening to me, these GREATS set the framework for how I would approach my entire life.

I am so grateful to my father for these lessons and give him credit for having the foresight to know these were lessons kids should hear too. I admit that, depending on my age, there were times I did not understand a great deal. But their teachings set me up with a mindset advantage that shaped my belief systems and helped me become the person I am today. I cherish the lessons these great men taught.

But let's get real. These greats were not teaching and directing their lessons to kids. They were men whose target listener was adult salesmen. I have long been searching for a woman to teach these concepts. And further, looking for anyone who had these amazing teaching programs that were directed at kids and teens. How amazing would it be to set up the world's children with a belief system that would help them become the most successful, happy people they could ever imagine! Here is what I have found:

- Two books written for teens to read:
  - » *Success for Teens* by the Success Foundation. I used this book in my

Student Leadership Program at the dance school and *Success Magazine* actually published a story on us! It was awesome and very inspiring to our students. The editor of the magazine at the time was Darren Hardy, who has since become one of my mentors and the one who actually told me it was time for me to write this book. Thank you Darren!

» The *7 Habits of Highly Effective Teens* by Sean Covey.

- One teaching curriculum that is specifically for high school teachers to implement called *Character Strong*. I highly recommend it for high schools. Our world would be a far better place if everyone learned how to treat one another kindly. This program has great success with this. We have adopted their philosophies at our school and recommend them to any schools that will listen!

- One year-long curriculum called *Star Leadership Program*, created by my amazing friend and fellow dance studio owner Tracy Wozney. She is making a difference in lives and it's incredible! I love her course and have used it at my studio's Teacher Assistant Leadership Program and we offer her course as a weekly class in our school.

- A few toddler books. My favorites are:
  - » *Have You Filled a Bucket Today* by Carol McCloud and David Messing
  - » *It's Not What You've Got* by Wayne Dyer

I bought them all and I have used them all. The amount of resources that go into training kids *how* to think is almost zero! It's well past time to pull together some kid-friendly strategies for moms to use to help their most precious commodity – their kiddos.

We moms spend hundreds and sometimes thousands of dollars a month to train our kids how to play soccer, dance ballet, and play the piano. Then we spend more on tutoring to catch our kids up academically or to give them a competitive edge. But we spend literally no time on their psyche unless there is a problem. Then we take our kids to a counselor or therapist. Have you tried going to a therapist? To many kids, this is somehow embarrassing and shameful. This idea needs to shift. Some churches have great children's programs and for that I am grateful. But where else are our children getting the thought process training? Oh, they are certainly getting some kind of training from YouTube. Do you know what it is? And many of us are blessed with incredible schoolteachers who value teaching about character as well as the value of high test scores. To be fair, schoolteachers have set curricula and limited time. By necessity, the focus is on memorizing class content. One of my close friends who is a teacher had her Vice Principal visit her classroom for an unannounced observation. A child was having a hard time so instead of sticking to the class lesson, she took the time to assist the one needy student. The result was not praise. It was the opposite. This is so sad. The VP focused on the lesson, rather than the child. This needs to change. Another book, right? But we can start with ourselves, by putting our child first.

Just as dance teachers, soccer coaches, and karate sensei's teach muscle memory for the body, and math teachers teach muscle memory for multiplication, we must teach muscle memory for how we think about living our life. Frankly, the earlier we start, the better. Serious ballet students train 4-6 days a week depending on their age. I am sure your daughter puts the same amount of time and energy into her passion. And how many hours a week do you specifically and intentionally put into your daughter's mindset training?

In this book you will find ways to help your daughter find her God-given gifts and her "why." Whatever her passion is, it will fuel her purpose. She needs your mentorship, the tools, and the time to do it. I have shared these principles with countless children over the years and watched them make dreams come true. Guess what ... because they wanted to be ballerinas or back up dancers in Hollywood, most grew and developed into amazing dancers, but not all of them went onto dance careers. The lessons and the process for becoming a great ballerina are the very same lessons that go into being a great anything.

Jenna Colin just sent me this text, many years after she graduated from our program:

"Ms. Neisha – I have some great news to share with you.... I was just offered my dream job at

ABC Medical Center for their Labor and Delivery/ Postpartum NEW Grad Residency Program. This has taken so many years to accomplish, and I wanted to let you know that you have played an important role in this. Your words of encouragement and endless support have helped me persevere ... I appreciate all of the hard work you have put into helping me gain confidence in myself to succeed in earning my dream job."

I am so proud of Jenna for finding her calling in life and staying persistent. Her gift is special. If you could see her face when she speaks about her love for delivering babies, you would see the light literally shining from her eyes. THIS. IS. Success! She reached her goal because she followed the SHINE process, even though she didn't necessarily know her goal would change from dancer to nurse. I want this for your daughter too.

I will share the concepts and techniques that we have seen work time and time again so that you too can put your children on the right track to live their best life and be their best self each and every day! Are you ready? Take my hand, Mom – let's go!

Chapter 3
Begin with the End in Mind
– What Is Your Dream?

*"My mom is my hero. [She] inspired me to dream when
I was a kid, so anytime anyone inspires you to dream,
that's gotta be your hero."*
– TIM MCGRAW

All right Mom, use your imagination for a moment with me ... you get in your car to drive to a special destination that you have never been to before. For the sake of discussion, let's use my own happy place, the beach. Do you drive aimlessly and hope you hit the water someday? No – that's not the woman's way. We instinctually get directions. In this day and age, we enter the destination into our GPS and follow the step-by-step navigation to get to where we want to go. Sometimes we take a wrong turn by accident – no biggie, we intentually redirect, get back on track, and continue getting closer to the beach. When we arrive at the sandy water's edge, we deeply inhale, breathing in the salty air. And we enjoy the sunshine and the view. With this concept in mind, we are going to begin with the end in mind. The Dream.

Newsflash. You bought this book to help your daughter, but in order to lead her you need to live the process yourself. So this is going to be your dream, not hers. We will help her with her dream next. Write your dream for yourself and your dream for your daughter down in your journal or on a post it note.

Here is my own example: my dream is to start a movement by equipping one million moms across the world to lead their daughter into a life of great love, great service, and great purpose.

My dream for my own girls is that each finds her God-given gifts in life and that the gift brings her great joy. I wish that she will develop that gift to her highest ability and then go on to share that with the world so that she has a sense of purpose and great worth in life. I dream that she will love others and feel the love from others and that she will know and love God.

Your turn.

My dream is:

_____

_____

_____

_____

_____

_____

My dream for my daughter is:

_____

_____

_____

_____

_____

_____

_____

Your daughter will need to write down her own Dream too. If she is working within our program, we will help her through that. If you are working through it at home and don't know your daughter's dream yet, you can begin when you are having quality time – say at the dinner table – by having a family discussion about dreams. Your daughter may know beyond a shadow of a doubt what her goal is. That's awesome. Let her have her dream any way she envisions it and let her imagine as many details as possible. The more clear the vision is, the better. I remember my ballet teacher was selling her studio when I was 15 years old. Obviously I was not going to buy it at age 15, but I spent hours and hours writing down every detail about how I would run the ballet studio and how I would grow it, if I did buy it. Seven years later, that school was gone, but I opened my own and all that dreaming got put into action.

But what if your daughter does not have a dream yet? Don't panic. Don't judge. Keep the conversation going in a positive way. Reframe the dinner question to, "What are some of the things you want for yourself?" This does not have to start an impactful dream, like "I want to be the first female president of the USA." What is important is to learn the process of how to think about and select a goal so it will become habit and therefore easier to attain when she has one that is important. She can start with, "I want to learn how to skateboard over the summer," "I want to move up to the middle level in math," or "I want to do magic in the talent show at school." Once you have something, ask your daughter to write down her Dream and post it on the bathroom or bedroom mirror. In my family, we put our dreams on a vision board so we can look at them every day.

Chris Hogan, one of the Dave Ramsey-school-of-thought teachers, says, "Dreams energize kids." And he is right. Ever ask a child, "What do you want for your birthday?" or "If you could fly anywhere, where would you fly to?" Kids' faces light up in anticipation and with great excitement that they cannot hold in, they giggle and, bursting at the seams, they literally blurt out their answer. Now think about what your daughter loves ... don't say YouTube or video games. Okay, yes, some people do make a living at YouTube and video games. One of my own children makes money on her YouTube channel! But, for the sake of this book, it has to be something your daughter loves. What is your daughter passionate about?

I believe that all of us were born with God-given gifts that are unique to each of us. Our job as people is to find out what our gifts are and share them with the world. The very act of sharing our gifts brings us deep satisfaction and fulfillment. Another more secular way to view this can be found in a statement by Mark Twain, "The two most important days in your life are the day you were born and the day you find out why you were born." Isn't that beautiful? Our hopes and our dreams are so often God calling us toward our gift. So, put that dream into your mental GPS as the goal. Whatever your daughter is drawn to and gets excited about is just fine, be it becoming a ballerina or a WBA basketball team Star (is that what it's called???).

GPS Your Dream

Kids like visuals so let's provide one for them. You can download our picture at www.shinegps.com (or have your daughter draw her own version). It's a picture of a road map or GPS. Make sure you print one for you and one for her. Let's put the grand destination aka: THE DREAM in at the end. Kids can draw a picture to go with it if they want. Most of the children I work with love dance, so I am putting a dance-related goal on the example. You will put your own goal on your GPS destination and have your daughter place her own BIG dream on her map. No judgment on your kid's dream. Remember I said that less than one percent of children are going to reach this exact long-term destination of being a professional ballerina? That is okay. Let your daughter have her own dream. I believed that becoming a ballerina was my dream. The pursuit of that dream led me to my ultimate calling of opening a dance school. Your daughter can and likely will change her mind, reroute, and U-turn. Remember that we are only in the beginning. AND the reason it's all okay is that learning the process to getting to their destination is the most important thing – not actually getting there as a child. But you are not going to tell her that! Just continue helping her work toward that destination. We tell our dancers that training is about the process, not the result.

But we do need to keep the desired result in mind so we keep going in the right direction. We will break it down into smaller, reachable, achievable goals along the way. Right now – think Big. End. Goal. One more note ... Mom, the goal on the GPS is not your goal for your daughter, it's her goal. For her to learn this process is MY ultimate goal and the reason you picked up this book, right? Let her put whatever goal she has into the destination. Let's go....

Download this SHINE GPS worksheet at www.shinegps.com.

Journaling

Misty Lown always says, "Think it, ink it." What she means is, when you have an important thought process or idea, it's important to get it out of your head ASAP and put it on paper. It's for this reason that I encourage journaling. It is one thing to think about a dream, but when you write down every detail on paper, your mind begins to visualize the outcome as reality. Your mind is an amazing thing. It will actually start working on how to overcome obstacles that are in your way and figure out how to make your visualized picture in your head a reality. It will work at it subconsciously in the same way that you would work on putting a puzzle together. Just like when I considered buying my teacher's dance studio. That was when my brain started to work on it. Years later, all the puzzle pieces fit, and a dance studio became my reality. Since most girls love journaling, I highly recommend that you pick up your daughter a cute or inspiring journal as a gift or order our SHINE journal from www.shinegps. com, and write her a love note in the front:

> *To my darling daughter,*
> *May all your dreams come true!*
> *Love, Mom*

Quick reminder: let your daughter see you journaling. You do not have to say anything about it. If a picture is worth a thousand words, then leading by example is worth a million!

So, now you and your daughter have destinations plotted on your road map and are hopefully writing about your goals in your journals. Remember, I will not get to my beach by jumping in the car, getting on the road, and hoping I will find the beach. I have to follow the directions until I memorize the path. Your daughter will need to follow the directions too. If she pushes back, take it slowly and keep leading by example. Sometimes getting the buy in from teens is difficult. Just acknowledge that there may be challenges and keep going. But for most at this point, we know where we are going and we are excited about it. We put in the starting point (wherever you are in life right now) and the end dream into the GPS. Next, we visualize.

Visualizations

Mom, take yourself back in your mind to the time you were asking your four-year-old version of your daughter about her birthday. Do you see her excited face? She transports herself immediately to be at the birthday party where all her friends are chanting her name, celebrating her, watching her open toy after toy, and eating sugar galore! She can visualize the glory of the moment so naturally at age four. And she is filled with so much joy, it's like she is actually at the party! Mom, you and I are going to tap into that gift of visualization and use it to help keep your daughter's eye on her own destination. When we visualize the Dream Come True, we are going to use all of our senses. We will see success, as it is occurring in the future, smell the smells, hear the sounds, and even taste if that's possible. The more realistic the vision, the better.

Here is the tip I learned from Peak Performance Athletes. Use the visualization technique as the last thing you do before bed. Then your mind will actually continue to review the vision as you sleep. If your children are little, you can lead this activity as a bedtime story. If your daughter is older, you can share the idea with her during your quality time and let her do it on her own. Here is an example that goes with the Ballerina sample:

Lily sees herself fully grown and on the side of the stage. She looks down and sees her beautiful hand-sewn costume and feels the rhinestones and appliqué on the bodice of the costume. Looking out at the audience, she sees the audience is full, she hears the familiar music, feels her hair pulled into a slick bun, and the shoes tightly wrapping her feet. She watches her fellow dancers take the opening position of the ballet. She can smell the stage – a dusty smell that is somehow comforting – and feel the warmth of the lights hitting her face. She knows the choreography, every step executed perfectly, she can feel how she interacts with other dancers, feel the sweat drip down the back of her neck, see her performance quality is matching the vision of the Director, and so on, and so on. The clearer the picture, the better.

The body drifts off to sleep but then the mind continues to rehearse, review, work out details, and analyze. This tip will have your daughter laser-focused on her dream. She can pick different dances, costumes, theaters, and so on. This strategy works for any sport, any career, any academics, public speaking, and so much more. Try it on yourself, Mom. Lie down and visualize every detail of your own dream as if it already were part of your here and now. When you tuck your daughter in at night, talk about this technique and encourage her to try it. The clearer the picture, the better. Jack Canfield, one of my mentors, says that the more emotionally connected you are during a visualization, the easier it is to get to the destination. So JUMP IN 100%. Try it and add visualization to your road map.

Chapter 4
Your Decision Lens

"Mama, you taught me to do the right things / So now you have to let your baby fly You've given me everything that I will need to make it through this crazy thing called life."
— CARRIE UNDERWOOD

Choices on the Road

Ever notice that there are a lot of choices on the road? Go through or stop at that yellow light? Swerve to go around the pothole? Give or not give an annoyed look to the mean guy who has been driving too close to your bumper and then speeds around you, only to stop at the same time as you at the light. Just like the real road, your daughter is going to have to make choices. Some will be made in the moment and some will be well thought out. Some decisions will not alter the destination and others will change the outcome dramatically and completely. Such is true with life. We moms always say, "We raised them the best we could and we just hope they make the right choices." Well, that sucks! Let's give our girls the tools for decision-making so when a decision matters, we can replace the words "just hope" above with "are confident." That is why you are reading this book, right? So let's continue on.

Our girls make a thousand little decisions every day. Meaningless choices like hairstyle and what shoes to wear have to be let go. These decisions get made without much thought, don't impact the world in any significant way, don't change her thought patterns or growth, and are not worth us investing time or arguing about. There are too many important decisions to care about, so we just have to let some of these petty things go. There are some decisions that ARE important. For example: our character, work ethic, and how we treat others. There it is, the Golden Rule. The Golden Rule matters. Treat others as you would like to be treated. The Golden Rule is how we moms teach our girls how to make the meaningful decisions count. And Mom, it starts with you role modeling for your daughter. Reminder, she is watching you all the time. How you treat the bagger at the grocery store, the way you speak to the teller at the bank, your gratitude toward her teachers, and your warm smiles to your daughter's friends are all showing her how a female should behave. As decisions for how to behave come up, intentionally decide to live by the Golden Rule. You are doing this for your daughter, but your life will end up changing for the better too. Teach your daughter by role modeling.

Earlier I told you that one of my decision lenses was family first. If you are not certain what your decision lens is, it's fun and easy to figure out. Do a quick Internet search for a list of values. Review them and pick the top ten that ring true as important. Then narrow that to the top three. These are the values that you make decisions with. This system has never failed me. When you do not know what to do, run your options through these value filters and boom, your decision is clear and you feel good about it. For example: if I am busy with a household project and my hubby says, "Let's take the kids to the beach," I run it through my filter. I want to finish the project and I am too busy tomorrow. If I leave, there will be a mess in the house for a week. BUT this opportunity to bond with my family is my decision-maker. The day that happened, I went to the beach and had the time of my life. No guilt for leaving the mess.

Time to share the concept with your daughter. Bring the values list to the dinner table and talk about them as a family. Let everyone pick his or her own top values – no judgment, please. Encourage everyone to put the values in a prominent place, like on a vision board, in a journal, or on a piece a paper taped to their bedroom wall as a visual reminder of what is important to them.

FAQs:

Q: Can I have more than three values?

A: Yes – We all DO have more than three values. For this exercise however, we are focusing on our top three at this stage of our life. If and when you change your values because you are in a different stage of life, no problem.

Q: Is it okay if my values change as I get older?

A: Yes. In fact, you can expect your values to change as you mature and go through different seasons of your life.

Put your top three values onto your GPS under Decision Lens. For the purposes of our example we will use Determination, Love, and Learning.

1 STARTING POINT
Me today

2 VISUALIZATION
Professional ballerina on stage

3 DECISION LENS
Your values: Determination, love, learning

Shine!
ROADMAP

12 DESTINATION
Professional Ballerina with Alvin Ailey

Align Your Circle of Influence: Organizations

You have identified your three most important core values. Now you must ensure that what surrounds you on the outside is reflective of these values. You are starting with the groups that you are in. For example:

- What does your school believe in?
- Do they walk the walk and talk the talk?
- Is it aligned with what you care about?
- What clubs are you in?

My own daughters came home from school with a permission slip to be in a club that painted their nails and watched a show called *Pretty Little Liars*. WHAT? NO WAY! My 6th grader does not need to see that trash! That is not a club for anyone in my family. (Side note: I took that one up with the teacher, who actually said she was taken aback by my shock. By the way, she didn't have kids.) On the other hand, my son takes soccer lessons from an incredible organization called Soccer Shots that has character building as part of their curriculum. Each week, the coach integrates a new character trait into their soccer lesson. I loved it so much that I borrowed the idea for our dance and music school. And now, it's a part of our own classroom culture.

Align yourself first. Yes Mom, you. Remember again, you set the example for your daughter. You choose who is a part of your life. Are you intentionally aligned with the people, groups, organizations, schools, coaches, friends, churches, clubs, stores, TV shows, podcasts, etc. that lead by the good example you wish she will follow? If not, take a hard look now and make some adjustments. Who you are and how you lead your life influences your child. So make your choices carefully. Your daughter is watching. Statistically, we humans are more likely to grow into whatever is surrounding us. Here is an example: I recently saw a post to a friend's Facebook page that was bitter, judgmental, short-sighted, and hurtful. I looked at this woman's child and guess what? She is bitter, judgmental, short-sighted, and hurtful. Is that the shining light you want your child to express? NO! You would not be reading this particular book if it were. Make your Circle of Influence list now.

1.

2.

3.

Some of my own organizations of choice are:

- My church: Helping people find and follow Jesus
- Rotary: Service above Self
- More than Just Great Dancing: We don't teach kids to make great dancers, we teach dance to make great kids!
- Character Strong: Cultivating a culture of character
- Youth Protection Advocates in Dance: Building empowered communities to keep youth happy, healthy, and safe in dance.

These are my faves based on my values and my career choice. They have become my tribes. The people in these groups support me, hold me accountable, and encourage me. Are your tribes in line with what you want to teach your daughter? If you have no organizations, it's time to actively search and find at least one that is in line with your life's passion and embraces what you value. Then align yourself with them.

Align yourself and your daughter will follow.

Dave Ramsey asks, "Who is leading the charge I am following?" I ask you Mama, WHO is leading the charge your daughter is following? Mom, hear me ... Dave says, "If you don't decide, someone else will" – like a stranger on YouTube! Gulp. SCARY! You cannot just "Hope." You are the kind of mother who will invest, influence, and direct your child. When she moves out and is on her own, then you can hope. But before that, align, align, align. Do not permit your children to follow a group, club, school, or activity that is not in alignment with your core values and beliefs. These are all choices and decisions on the road to our destination.

This can be frustrating for Moms, especially if they have teens that have been making their own poor decisions for a while. In my program, I speak directly with the teens in a safe space.

It's effective because it is not Mom telling them what to do. It's me leading them through an exploration exercise, allowing them to make the connections for themselves and actively choose to try the Shine system on their own accord. You can do this yourself Mom, but you may need to be sneaky about it. Choose your timing. In the teen years as girls seek their independence from you, it can get tricky for your kids to hear you. (That makes it sound so nice! – okay – truth, sometimes teenage girls don't listen and don't care!) So when you are bringing these decisions up about groups that align with your values, talk about YOU, not your daughter. This way you are inviting her into the concept and conversation, not judging her or forcing change on her.

Once you have her buy in, you can talk as a family about everyone's different tribes. The family dinner is a great time and place to have all these discussions because the focus is not on your daughter. It will not feel like a magnifying glass of judgment is on your daughter, which can make her run. Here the conversation can be shared with the other parent, grandparents, other siblings, etc.

Your daughter will step into healthy tribes, groups, or organizations when she wants to. But just like you can lead a horse to water, but cannot make them drink, you are leading your daughter to the map, but she must actually be the one to follow the directions.

Add at least one group to your own GPS before you move on. Have your daughter add a group to her GPS as well.

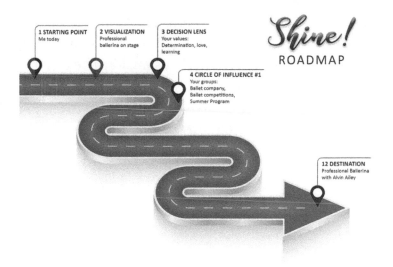

Align with Your Five Friends

When you are ready to take it up a notch, add this next section. Please don't dive into it all at once. You need to create the buy in before you can take your daughter to the next important level, which is: the top five friends in her life. This is her life and she needs to OWN it by surrounding herself with people she admires and aspires to be like. There are good people who can and will help her to go in the direction she wants to go. But wait … (You knew this was coming, Mom) … who do we start with? Ourselves. Read this section and do the work for yourself, then share it with your daughter.

It is well known that we become like the top five people we hang out with. So, stop right now and list your top 5. Next to each of your five names, rate them on how they treat others and note what they care about.

1.

2.

3.

4.

5.

If their goals and values are in line with your own values and goals, this is someone you should keep around you. If not, it is time to kindly move on. If these five people are smarter, more generous, more grateful, or basically ahead of you in where you want to go – stick with these people. You will learn and grow with them. If your friends are not in harmony with how you want to live your life or with your goals, kindly move on. Looking at it from the opposite side, the influence of bad friends is like a sneeze: the germs spread quickly and can take you down when you are not expecting it.

Next, have your daughter create her list. If she does not do it on her own, you can likely guess who are the five people she spends the bulk of her time with. Carefully consider the names on your daughter's list. Do you want your child to become more like these people? Just like you did on your own exercise, rate the friends on how they treat others and notate what they care about. Do they live by the Golden Rule, study hard, obey the rules, volunteer, try to improve their physical skills or themselves in some way? If yes, then that is a good friendship. If the answers are no or worse – they are qualities that you never want your child to have – minimize that friendship ASAP. You may ask how to do that. It can be tricky. Younger kids will usually just follow your instructions. But with teens it is hard to tell. The best advice is to start the SHINE process when your kids are young so it is already ingrained into their psyche. If they are older and resistant to your advice on friends, they must do the work on their own so they can see for themselves and make their decisions themselves. A therapist or Youth Pastor can help. Working directly with us in our SHINE program will help as well. You can walk your daughter through this lesson but remember, if you do not have her buy in, she will run toward the friends you want her to back off from. Start with laying the foundation by openly working on yourself and sharing. You can ask her if she ever thought about this. When she is ready, she will make her own list. Know that the five friends she surrounds herself with most are one of the largest decisions she will ever make on the road toward her destination. These kids will have the power to encourage her and support her, or tear her down and distract her. Her choices matter because decisions turn into results. Add your friends and your daughter's friends to the GPS.

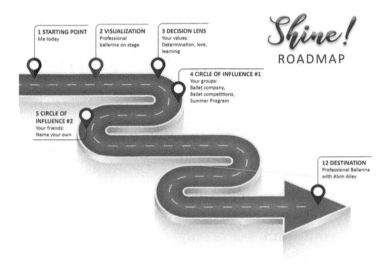

Align with Your Coaches and Teachers

Another major influence on your daughter's life is her primary coach or teacher. If your daughter wants to be a superstar, you must search out a top coach. If she wants to be a violinist, you need a real music teacher who knows the process and can instruct you on the many demands of a music career, hold her accountable, and offer her opportunities for growth. Whatever her team, art, or group is, you must believe in the vision, system, or processes of her leader. If you do not, MOVE ON QUICKLY. "But this coach trains all the best." So what? If they are not in alignment with your core values, it doesn't matter who they know or how many careers they have launched. Your daughter may follow more than the skill she is learning. Make sure the leader your daughter is following is leading her where you want her to go in skill and in character. That is on you. I am not telling you anything new – there are amazing coaches who will help train your daughter's talent AND shape her character; and then there are wolves in coach's clothing. YOU have to evaluate who is a good coach, based upon your value system.

At the dance studio, one of the most important jobs I have is selecting the teachers who will interact with our students. This is similar to what you are doing when you select a coach for your own daughter. So I want to walk you through the process. After I have confirmed that an applicant has the required expertise and experience, I focus on their character. I check them out on social media and I look for confirmation that they are or are not a match for our school's culture. Not sure? Ask them what is important to them in life. If you listen long enough, people will tell you everything you need to know. Next is a background check. Only if all this looks good does a person get to meet our students. These people are going to be influencers and you better believe they are hand-selected because they are amazing and have something special to offer in addition to their art. If at any time that amazingness fades or they fall short – they are OUT OF HERE. They do not get to be influencers of my students any more. Once you have pinpointed who you are picking as an influencer for your daughter, build relationships with them and respectfully communicate.

Side note of advice: once you have selected your coach and your daughter is working with them, do not presume that it's acceptable to tell the coach how to do their job. If you do not like how they are doing things, move on. Complaining, telling the coach how you would want things done, making special requests on behalf of your child, etc. are all inappropriate. You have paid for the expertise of the coach, so let them do their job. I know you would not yell at or belittle a brain surgeon while she is operating on your daughter's brain! You would want the surgeon to be laser-focused. So give your child's coach the same respect!

Look at your own coaches. Do you have a personal trainer? Pastor? Mentor? Financial advisor? Attorney? List them here:

1.

2.

3.

4.

5.

Ponder your list. Are your teachers in alignment with the mission and vision you have for your life? If not, you know what to do ... kindly move on. Repeat the exercise, listing your daughter's coaches and mentors below. If there are none, you can fix it immediately. Talk to your daughter, find something she likes to do, and sign up for a class to help her improve at it. Not sure what to do? Start at the YMCA or Parks and Recreation. These places have pages and pages of classes and opportunities that are fairly reasonably priced. Or start making stops at various activities to check them out and see what sparks your daughter's interest.

Your daughter's coaches/teachers:

1.

2.

3.

4.

5.

Now add the coaches to the GPS.

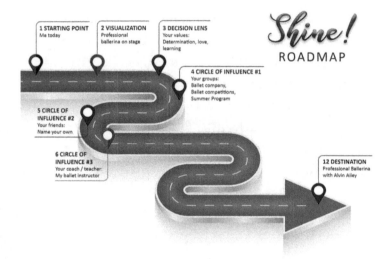

Chapter 5
How You Treat Yourself Speaks Loudly

"I am a strong woman because a strong woman raised me."
– UNKNOWN

L isten to yourself talk for a while. When you think of others, is it complimentary or complaining? Is it generally positive? Critical? Downright hateful? Give yourself an honest evaluation. You can monitor yourself for a few hours and determine where your thought patterns are. Next, listen to your self-talk. What do you say to yourself? What do you think about yourself? When that little voice inside is talking to you, is it kind, supportive, and problem solving, or cynical, name-calling, and hurtful?

Why are we doing this exercise? Because scientists know that what you think about, you become. I often wonder why this is not well known. Further, why is it not taught by schoolteachers? Henry Ford said, "Whether you think you can or think you can't, you're right." That is because your brain does not decipher if you are right or wrong in how you talk to yourself; either way, *your brain will believe you*. So, please talk nicely to yourself. You are driving yourself crazy with all the nastiness you say in your mind about yourself and others! Your brain believes the negative and then sets out to prove you are right. You must intentionally think and say nice things about yourself.

Let's write five generous and loving compliments about yourself here:

1.

2.

3.

4.

5.

If this is a challenge for you, I would like to suggest you get some assistance. There is an entire industry dedicated and available to you: that is, to mantras. Head over to amazon.com and search mantras to find both books and audio guides that will lead you through positive affirmations and meditations. I bought a magazine called *Mantras and Meditations* (there's no way my teen girls will read a book right now!) and I left it in the bathroom for my daughters to flip through. In our SHINE program, we spend significant time on this topic. It can be truly transformational. After the initial, "This is weird" thoughts, speaking nicely to yourself will become a normal, very healthy habit. Rise to the occasion, Mom ... this is YOUR LIFE! What if it does not work, you ask? So what – what have you lost? You got this far in the book because you trust me. Annnnndddd of course, remember your daughter is watching, always watching and listening, and repeating. If you are spewing negativity and coldness, guess who is also spewing negativity and coldness? Yep, your daughter is. Do you want that for her?

On that note, let's turn the conversation toward your daughter. Not sure how she talks to herself? Listen for a while to see if you can pick up on anything. Listen to how she talks to others and listen to what she says about herself in general conversation. Generally speaking, the younger she is, the easier it is to figure out. For teens, you'll have to ask questions and engage in conversation to get clues. Many teens have a culture of being negative. In fact, I got an education in this recently when my two teenage girls and I went to an unnamed popular retail store for girls. It turns out that everything in the store is one size. First of all, what the heck is that? You fit the one mold or you don't fit in? Second of all, never mind. I digress from my point, which is: I sat in the car for a few minutes and watched the clones – er, teen girls – approaching the store. One hundred percent of the people entering the store had on a sour face. I mentioned to my daughters, "Do you notice that everyone looks disgusted? Is something wrong? What's the deal?" My girls said to me, "That's not disgust, mom. It's pouty. It's the look." I kid you not! An entire EXPENSIVE brand of used-looking clothing that only comes in one size is famous for its customers being in a bad mood ... and they're thriving. I drove forty-five minutes to get to this store so that my children could be a part of this!? Well, if you are getting to know me at all through this book, you can imagine that I left that wasted trip quite frustrated at our world. This is definitely not what I want for my own children OR yours!

Talk to your daughter about what she values in herself. Help her create her list. Put the list up in a prominent place, like her bedroom door. In our SHINE training, we offer several activities to encourage students to focus on self-talk. We work through this process of identifying the positive things kids can personally say about themselves. One beautiful concept that we adopted from Leslie Scott of Youth Protection Advocates in Dance (YPAD) is called Spirit Swag Week. Students of all ages, in every class, gather in a circle and share with one another something great about themselves. The kids receive Spirit Swag Buttons, provided by YPAD. The whole point is to start the kids thinking positively about themselves and make it a normal part of life. After the class we give them a button, usually to put on their dance bag, as a visual reminder to continue to remember what they believe is awesome about themselves. You can adapt this in your own home by buying a special pin (these are so popular right now!) for your daughter's backpack, as a reminder of what she loves about herself.

Another exercise we use came from an attorney, Carl A. Grubb. This kind man once presented me with a beautiful mirror that had a saying etched in it. The purpose of the mirror is to look into it at yourself while reading the inscription at the same time. Here is what it said:

"I love you.
I will always treat you as the Magnificent Being you are.
I am your best friend forever."

We adopted this at the dance studio, too. We have our students stare at themselves in the classroom mirror and say an affirming phrase like this one out loud. At first, some age groups are giggly and uncomfortable with this exercise. (How sad that they are uncomfortable being kind to themselves!) Luckily that passed and the students now take this seriously. It is impactful and beautiful. And you too can modify this idea for your own daughter. For example: you can buy your own mirror (or use the bathroom mirrors) and use dry erase markers to write different notes, affirmations, or words of encouragement. I put the mirror up by my front door and every once in a while, on our way out the door, I stop to role model what to do in the mirror. I don't say that that's what I'm doing, I just do it. I know my four kids are watching. After introducing some of these concepts at home, the whole family can have a conversation about self-talk. Catch each other in positive talk and remind one another when you hear it turn negative. I also rotate bathroom mirror mantras. The first time I wrote on the bathroom mirrors, my kids were shocked. But it's no biggie. It wipes right off if you use the right marker. Now my kiddos look forward to the little love notes.

Now fill in your own and your daughter's GPS with "Talk nicely to myself" and give yourself a compliment while you do it.

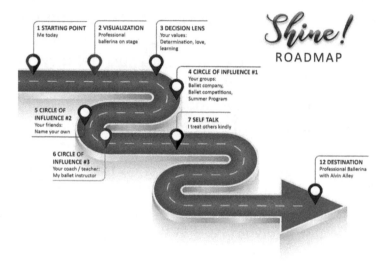

Chapter 6
Gratitude

*"Gratitude is the healthiest of all human emotions.
The more you express gratitude for what you have, the more
likely you will have even more to express gratitude for."*
– Zig Ziglar

Y ou and I have heard many stories about the
kids in third world countries like Haiti and
Uganda. These kids have nothing. Any attention,
education, fresh water, or clothing is received with
overwhelming happiness and gratitude. Any gift is
special and cherished because these children know
a life without a healthy diet, without clean water,
without shoes, without an education, and often

without parents. You may even know people who have started non-profit programs or gone over to serve and help. I have donated to many programs and have enlisted the help of our students to join me in raising money and awareness. We will come back to this in the next chapter to discuss how serving others is important. For now, we are looking at the third world experience to shine a light on how our children are so very fortunate. These days, our own children are often sheltered from this harsh reality. For example, most of the children in the United States do not wonder if they will have clean water to drink today or if they will have a blanket when they sleep. They take these things for granted – as do I. Jump into the mind of our own daughters and we see they are wondering if they should wear their high tops or low tops today and which of their many favorite Starbucks drinks they should order. I am not saying that having wealth is a bad thing. It is not. Our girls are innocent because they have not experienced such a level of extreme poverty. We thank God every day for this incredible blessing. But since most of our daughters have not had this life experience that teaches gratitude, perhaps some perspective is in order. In the name of wanting the best for our sweet girls, we moms have accidentally started the "ME" mindset, and it has become one of the parenting challenges that we face. Kids do not like to be labeled as entitled, but the reality is, so many of them are. Nobody wants to subject their babies to an impoverished life, so we need to find ways to teach our children how to be grateful.

Once again, being grateful begins with you. Demonstrate an intentional outward expression of gratitude for anything and everything so that your daughter will learn this habit. What are you grateful for? When can you share your gratitude? Here are samples:

Walk out the front door and say – "I am so grateful for [fill in the blank]."

Is it snowing? Say "my warm jacket," "the four seasons," or "we get to get into a car with heat."

Or is it sunny outside? Say, "the vitamin D from the sun," "the flowers blooming," "the sun for warming the swimming pools … let's go swimming today!"

Moms, you can show gratitude about literally ANYTHING. And we must. The pouty-face teen culture is out there and they want our daughters – and spend loads of money to get them. Don't let them take over!

Research shows us that the power of gratitude is impactful. On happierhuman.com we learn that gratitude makes us happier, makes others like us more, makes us healthier, boosts our careers (or in our kids' cases, their academics and sports/arts), strengthens our emotions, develops our personality, reduces materialism, increases spiritualism, makes us less self-centered, increases self-esteem, helps us live longer, increases energy, makes us more likely to exercise, and the list goes on and on and on! This is research-based, not a personal opinion. If one emotion can do so much good for us then we need to run, (not walk) toward gratitude and share it with anyone who will listen – most importantly, our children. Even if you are doubtful, you have nothing to lose by trying it.

As usual, let's begin with you. Start by brainstorming a list of what you are grateful for. Go!

_____

_____

_____

_____

_____

_____

_____

_____

_____

_____

Using your list as a reference, put reminders around your home, office, car, wherever you hang out. You can use sticky notes, dry erase boards, framed artwork, whatever. Put these up as reminders so that you can see and think of them often. You know what you are grateful for, you see it, you feel it. The next step is showing it.

Here are some more ideas for sharing your gratitude (remember to let your children see you):

- Write notes of gratitude to people: anyone and everyone you are grateful for.
- Use your words to speak your gratitude to anyone.
- Journal about your gratitude
- Prayer: tell God what you are grateful for.

Back at the dinner table, the safe place to have a conversation that does not feel entirely directed at your daughter, share the research with the family. This may spark a conversation about how cool the concept is. Ask if anyone at the table ever noticed any of this gratitude stuff to be true. You know now that role modeling is always the best strategy. Let your children see you expressing a heart full of gratitude to others and also to them. Catch them doing good works. Tell them in any way you can think of that you noticed and love them. If your daughter does the dishes, hug her and say how much you appreciate her help. If she opens the door for an elderly person, write her a note on her bathroom mirror that you saw her being kind and how it fills your heart with gratefulness that she is your daughter. Pay attention to all that is good about her and tell her often about the good characteristics that you see and why you are grateful. One sentiment I have adopted and share with all my kids is, "Out of all the kids in the whole wide world, I am so grateful that God brought you to me and that you are my child." Take that, memorize it, and say it often. It will make your daughter feel like she is worth a million bucks – and she is! And what's more, it will make you feel like a million bucks, too.

My mentor, Darren Hardy, shares that he once did an entire gratitude journal dedicated to his wife. Every day for a year, he wrote something he was grateful to her for. After a year, he gave this journal to her as a gift and says it was a game-changer in his marriage. I thought it was so beautiful and deeply meaningful that I have started my own journal to my husband. My journal is spanning several years. I have not given him the journal and he does not know it exists (okay – he will after he reads this!). But I am so excited about the day I will give him the filled-up book. Try it yourself.

At the studio, we teach gratitude in many ways. In fact, it has become a part of our daily culture. For example: at the end of class, kids will curtsey, bow, or applaud for their teacher. If a Master Teacher or Choreographer is visiting our students, the kids approach the guest and look them in the eyes with a smile and say, "Thank you." During the week before Thanksgiving, the dance and music classes stop for ten minutes so that all students in every class can reflect and write down what they are thankful for. They write on small paper leaves and then we create Gratitude Trees with the leaves. It's a beautiful tradition to experience. We follow up during the Valentine's Season. We invite the parents into class with us and we repeat this exercise with heart shaped papers that we post all over the walls! You can do this at home with your own gratitude tree. Both you and your daughter add something you are grateful for each day of November or something you love each day in February.

The students in our leadership program go even further during February. Ericka Moore, our leader, has them secretly deliver notes and small gifts of appreciation to the staff. I can tell you that it is a deeply impactful thing. The first time we did this, at least half of my staff mentioned it to me as a highlight in their life. I did not tell the staff that it was going to happen and the teachers were surprised and delighted by the love and appreciation. It was beautiful to watch! Now, it's a normal part of life for our students to express their gratitude. I keep the sweet notes they write me in a special place in my office because these genuine words remind me why I have dedicated my life to teaching children. Here is one sweet note that I have held onto.

> Ms. Neisha,
>
> Thank you for everything you do for us. Thank you for helping me to be a great dancer. You teach us morals such as respect, gratitude, and responsibility. You teach us to be respectful by showing us to be nice to our teammates. You show us to have gratitude by being respectful to our teachers. You show us to be responsible by teaching us to remember our things and to bring them to be prepared for dance. You make us better people.
>
> With love, Paulette
> 2016

Let's add gratitude to both your and your daughter's GPS.

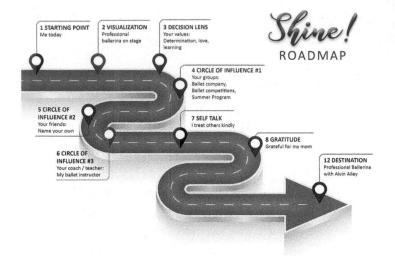

Chapter 7
Service

*"Thousands of candles can be lighted from a single
candle, and the life of the candle will not be shortened.
Happiness never decreases by being shared."*
– BUDDHA

I have a yearly tradition called Lunch with a Leader
where I take my Leadership Team to lunch with
one of the strong female leaders in our community.
We have shared meals with the Mayor, the Head of
the Library, the Chamber of Commerce CEO, and
many more. When these women share their hearts
with us, we learn how to be better women and
better leaders ourselves. Several years back, we met

with a leader who is the president of a local bank and a volunteer in our community. When we asked her about what made her successful, she shared her story. And here is the abbreviated version:

She came from humble beginnings. She grew up in Tijuana, Mexico. Tijuana is only about five miles from where I live in the United States. While there are very wealthy sections of Tijuana, she came from the area where life is rife with poverty, social upheaval, and a shortage of everything. I went into this area to do a home build project. I saw with my own eyes that just across the border, there are whole communities of people who live in one-room homes made from five garage doors pushed together. There is no running water, limited electricity, and dirt floors. It is a reality that is hard to see. Our leader made her way to America and through persistence, love of God, and a heart of service, she worked her way up to where she is today. It is she who encouraged me to join the Rotary, whose motto is Service above Self.

The Rotary taught me that serving others is a way of life. I have learned from my fellow Rotarians' example that the more we serve, the more our hearts grow. And so with this in mind, I encourage you to find ways to serve in your own community. There are many service-oriented groups you can join and most churches have connections with numerous outreach programs. Your kid's school is always looking for help (and that's a great way to get to know the leaders and build relationships with the people who influence your kids). Or you can Google "nonprofit organizations near me." You will find lists of organizations that need help. Find one that speaks to you and donate your time and talents. This is one of those "lead by example" moments, Mom. Your daughter is watching.

Mom, you have probably done the exercise where you envision yourself on your deathbed and look back at your life. Do you think you will be more proud of the fact that you spent all of your time focused on your hair, your makeup, your outfit, your diamonds, and your clean car OR that you spent your days helping lift up other people, holding the door for others to pass before you, smiling at the cashier in front of you, sorting food for the hungry, sending money for fresh water in Uganda, etc., etc., etc.? You know, Mom, you can still have a nice outfit and a clean car AND serve others.

After you lead by example and chat about your experiences with the family, invite your daughter to join you. I took two of my daughters to the Tijuana home building project with me. Talk about an eye-opening opportunity to give them some perspective! My emotions are caught in my chest just remembering the experience. I also volunteered all four kids to do trash pickup along one of the busiest streets in our town. It was hot, dirty, and exhausting. We found things you don't want to find! BUT, it was also incredibly rewarding to make a positive impact. Together, we made a difference to our city and together we made an incredible memory. Oh, I am sure my teens don't see it that way now. It was probably pure torture at the time. But my priority is the character that these experiences teach and that I am nurturing and developing in them.

I give great credit to Leslie Scott of YPAD for helping us launch service as a part of our studio's normal culture. Among other things, she is a holistic hip-hop teacher. She came to the studio to teach hip-hop and took our dance teams and their parents to serve at Feeding San Diego. We sorted fruit that would go into backpacks for children to take home from school on Friday, so they would have healthy food options for the weekend. That first experience stirred something in me. And now serving is a way of life for our students. We have all sorts of opportunities for our students to get involved with kids helping kids. We have raised money for Canines for Kids, collected gift baskets for Samaritan's Purse, and repeatedly performed in a benefit show to raise money for A Night to Remember Prom Organization, to name a few. Make service a way of life for yourself and for your daughter.

Now add service to each of your GPSs.

1 STARTING POINT
Me today

2 VISUALIZATION
Professional
ballerina on stage

3 DECISION LENS
Your values:
Determination, love,
learning

Shine!
ROADMAP

4 CIRCLE OF INFLUENCE #1
Your groups:
Ballet company,
Ballet competitions,
Summer Program

**5 CIRCLE OF
INFLUENCE #2**
Your friends:
Name your own

7 SELF TALK
I treat others kindly

8 GRATITUDE
Grateful for my mom

**6 CIRCLE OF
INFLUENCE #3**
Your coach / teacher:
My ballet instructor

9 SERVICE
Open door for
others every time.

12 DESTINATION
Professional Ballerina
with Alvin Ailey

Chapter 8
Habits

"YOUR CHOICE (decision) + BEHAVIOR (action) +
HABIT (repeated action) + COMPOUND (time)
= GOALS."
– DARREN HARDY

Have you heard that what you do, you become? If you spend your time with your family, you are family-focused. If you spend your time at the gym, you are physically fit. If you spend your time smoking dope, you are a dope head. You will reap what you sow, Mom. We must create habits that we can successfully repeat every day so that the habit becomes our norm. You have habits already. You brush your teeth so you don't get cavities, you put a jacket on so you do not get cold, and you pack your water bottle, etc. Your habits will become your daughter's unconscious habits as well. To get your mind around it, let's list some habits that you love that you do or you would like to start. Example: I walk thirty minutes a day and we have a family dinner six out of seven days a week.

- My Good Habits:
- Habits I want to start:

You also might have habits you want to give up. Example: Drinking soda at lunch and watching the news after dinner.

- My Habits to Give Up:

When you create a new habit and start to make it a part of your life, I recommend sharing it with someone who will support you – a friend, a spouse, a doctor, a trainer, or an accountability partner. The reason being, when you work with another person on your habit, it's harder to let yourself off the hook. One of the habits I began this year with my husband is waking up at 5 a.m. to sit together and listen to the Daily Audio Bible. Last year, I tried to listen on my own while I was walking. After six weeks, I had several excuses – I had to travel, I overslept and did not get my walking time, the Old Testament is too hard to read, and so on. But with my husband, I am motivated to sit and focus. Plus I get to snuggle with him without any little ones needing our attention!

It takes time to set a new habit. Some researchers say it takes 21 days. More recent statistics say it takes 66 days! And Jack Canfield says that if you skip a day, you have to start back at day one again. (That's so frustrating to me!) If a good habit takes time to create, it's worth it, regardless of the amount of time it takes. So just start again. The same is true for the habits you are trying to break. I recall a time when I cut sugar from my life. I learned very quickly that it was easier to cut out sugar completely cold turkey than to try to slowly eat less of it.

Now that you are leading by example, look to your daughter's habits. What are some of the habits she has? Does she eat an apple every day? Spend three hours on the Internet every day? Read each night before bed? Whatever you observe, notate for yourself only. Later, not in the moment, spend some quality time with her and discuss it. If she knows what she wants to excel at and what her dream is, discuss what she thinks she needs to do to achieve her dream. Whatever list she comes up with will be her habits and then these habits become her action steps that she can take to get closer and closer to her dream. She can write them down and check them off her list. It is a good idea to meet with her coach/teacher to help identify if her list of habits is right on or needs to be adjusted. I recently had a dance student who began taking dance class as a senior in high school. She took two hours a week and seriously thought she was going to become a professional back up dancer in Hollywood. She needed a loving reality check on her habits. This training regime will not get her to her destination. Pull in the experts in your daughter's life to help her create the habits that will take her to her dream come true. And that is the ultimate goal; to have intentional habits that take her in the direction she wants to go, rather than habits that lead her to feeling like a victim of life.

Need suggestions on how to lovingly steer your daughter toward good habits? Well, first off – if she is excited about her dream, she will be excited about most of her habits. But sometimes, it can be tough. The draw of YouTube, video games, and fast food addictions can be strong. My advice is to get out in front of it. One friend has an app on her child's electronics that literally turns the game off after 30 minutes. Perfect. Or, turn off the Internet, or go to the store ALONE so the begging and pleading for ice cream and chips doesn't persuade you. Pack a healthy snack instead of stopping for fast food. It's all habits, Mom. Kids may have a temper tantrum and put up a fuss. But it will be temporary. Hold steady.

Now, plug these habits into your daughter's SHINE GPS. In addition to these, notice that every step in our book is becoming a learned habit that will help take her to her final destination.

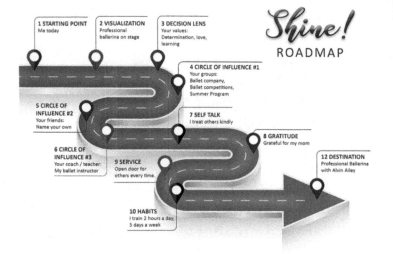

Chapter 9
Road Block:
What do I do now?

"Lessons often come dressed up as
detours and roadblocks."
– OPRAH WINFREY

Annoying roadblocks. They show up unannounced, take you by surprise, and cause you to lose time (a mom's most valuable resource). Roadblocks happen in real life too. Best advice, know they are going to happen sometimes and when they do, stay calm! We women are notorious for getting emotional and while it is okay to feel what you feel, it is a whole lot easier to navigate a roadblock with a clear head. Here's the thing: sometimes, the obstacles that come up are actually learning and growing opportunities. Here are some dance industry examples: the students are all on stage performing and the music cuts out. It's a typical technical difficulty. Do you freak out, screaming at the teacher? Some have! But no – it happens – it's life. The kids can stay on stage and finish the dance without music, showing how well they know their choreography (or don't) with no beat to hold them together. Or, for whatever reason, one of the students doesn't show up to a performance. Do you flip out? Gossip? Loads of moms do. No. The students learn how to adjust on the spot, in the moment. Sound like good life skills? They sure are. Instead of being angry because of these problems, look at what our kids are learning by facing the obstacle or challenge head on. In either of these cases, our children might fail. And? So what? When did it become bad to let little girls fail? Mom, look back at your upbringing. Did you fail? The choir sings all together: "YEEESSSSS." You are reading this book, so I know you want the very best for your daughter. Sometimes it is the best thing for her to fail. Failure teaches us. Failure can fuel us. And failure again will soon bring success. Abraham Lincoln lost eight elections, twice failed in business, and suffered a nervous breakdown. All of these seeming failures taught him persistence and endurance. Nobody wishes that their daughter will face hardship, but when it comes – and it will – let her learn how to handle the emotions and gain resilience. She will learn the strategies for navigating around the roadblock. Don't shield and protect her from the opportunity for growth.

Michael Jordan, arguably one of the best basketball players of all time, says, "During a game I don't compete with the other team or anybody else. I compete with my best work so far." Every day he is working to be the next best version of himself. Pause to think about that. Now weigh that against what is instinctual in kids. I hear chanting, "I am better than you are." There's even a funny song dedicated to it called, "I can do anything you can do, better." You want to be the best at something? Learn from someone who IS the best, Mr. Jordan. We moms must share this lesson with our daughters. We don't need to be the best this, that, or the other. We need to strive to be OUR best or to progress from OUR best. So often we see kids (or MOM's) get competitive and try to keep up with the Jones' daughter. If the Jones' daughter won a trophy, my daughter should win a trophy. If the Jones' daughter got promoted, my daughter should be promoted. That's not how life works, Mom! Not everyone gets every job and not everyone gets accepted to every college. We need to teach our kiddos how to cope with disappointment in a healthy way. Set your daughter's mindset to focus on what she is getting out of her experience, not on how she compares to others who are also getting the experience. Make sure your mindset is focused on this too. And if your daughter does not like her outcome (never mind what anyone else's outcome is) then she should work to change her outcome.

Another way to say this is to help your daughter Stay in her Own Lane. Help your daughter focus on herself. For example: help her sell as many Girl Scout cookies as she can so that she has contributed to the mission and vision of Girl Scouts, and leave it at that. Don't compete against the other girls selling cookies, no matter the prize. Or, in dance class – don't focus on the person standing next to you. Who cares what level they are? Remind your daughter to focus on her own progress and on what she is learning. If you spend your life comparing yourself, there is always going to be someone better at something and that comparison game takes too much time away from one working on oneself and enjoying life. It also perpetuates negative self-talk, which we now know is a no-no.

This month, my six-year-old enrolled in a tap class. Afterwards, she shared that a girl in the class leaned over and said, "I am better than you." My six-year-old kept her mouth shut, thinking "It's my first day – of course you are better than me if you have been here for a while." But it bothered her enough to tell me there was a mean girl in class. My thought – ROAD BLOCK! My daughter and I talked about the kind things she could have said back, like, "Yes – you are so good at tap! I am lucky to stand by you so I can learn." Just say something nice with a smile and it's over. Between us moms, the mean child probably does not have a mom like the moms reading this book, who are teaching their daughters how to focus on themselves, while remaining supportive of those around them.

One of the things that automatically happens nowadays when we hit a detour in the road is that our GPS reroutes us. There's no spastic frustration – you simply follow a new path. No wasted energy or breath. The GPS is your guide. You follow it. Our daughters are used to that. So when you hit a roadblock, keep your cool and let your daughter see you adjust and get going again. When our girls hit bumps in the road, we must teach them what to think. "Oops, learned from that one, re-route, and keep going."

One phrase that we use in our house is, "Thanks for the reminder." Whenever one of us gives another a gentle nudge that it's time to re-route we say, "Thanks for the reminder." That way there is no anger, no guilt, nobody is less-than or greater-than. Try it the next time your daughter reminds you of some annoying mistake you made. And, add the roadblock to both of your GPS maps.

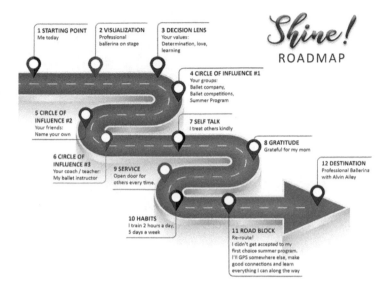

Chapter 10
Closing

"Do the best you can until you know better.
Then when you know better, do better."
– MAYA ANGELOU

Maya Angelou lived through many liberating seasons in America. She observed and contributed to the equal opportunity strides women have made in the last 70 years. Because of this, I have a book of her poetry in our home. I want my daughters to know great influencers like Maya Angelou. I also keep *O, The Oprah Magazine* hanging around, and *Chicken Soup for the Kids and Teens* books. Who are your favorite influencers?

What kind of magazines and books do you have lying around your home that your girls will pick up and flip through? Do a five-minute check and fix this right now.

When we began the journey, we established that your daughter wants the world on a platter – and hurry up about it! Maybe she wants to be a ballerina or a back-up dancer; maybe it's a basketball star or a doctor, or a hundred other goals. The actual destination of where your daughter wants to go is irrelevant to the end point of this book. Because the goal of life is not the destination at all, it is the journey. When she learns her calling, loves others, is grateful, living life fully, and serving others along the way, this is how your daughter will reach her destination. If she does these things, your daughter will be happy and thriving and that will bring you the greatest happiness any mom can ever feel.

I encourage you to surround your daughter and indeed your entire family with uplifting things. For example, post the family mantra at the front door and say it out loud each time you leave for the day. Don't have one? There are hundreds available online. Use one you like or create your own. Put it on paper and tape it to the wall, frame it, or paint it on. My own kids love this morning tradition and will remind me when I forget.

My friend Darcy shared this tip with me: in the car on the way to school, before listening to your favorite jam, take three minutes to listen to a quick podcast. My personal favorite is called The Darren Daily – it's a daily mentoring video that gets texted right to my phone at 5 a.m. each day. It's not specifically directed at kids but it's got big picture concepts that kids can grab onto. And these days, podcasts are a dime a dozen. Find a good one that speaks to you and your daughter and start listening today.

I also encourage you and your daughter to keep your "why" in front of you. If your inspiration is close at hand, it will help you to keep your focus. On the recommendation of one of my friends, my own family just spent Easter Day making Vision Boards. Our many goals and inspirations are all on big poster boards that are boldly posted in our home. Unlike the road map that shows the behaviors for how to get to your one Big Dream, the Vision Board can have lots and lots of dreams. Mine has professional goals, like I want to publish this book.

And, it also has my dream vacation destination and my dream location for a home, etc. It's helpful to us because we now see our dream destinations repeatedly throughout the day. And that is a good thing because it's very hard to get anywhere if you don't know you want to go there.

I want to close by sharing an email I just received from a Mom. Warning: get out your tissues. One of my ten-year-old students who has gone through the SHINE process since age three wrote the following speech. She went on to win her school speech contest. I am so proud of her – not for winning the contest, but for winning at life! Through the pursuit of her goal (and by the way, she is a fabulous young dancer too), she has overcome her challenges and come away joyfully wanting to help others. That is what I want for your daughter, that is what I want for you, and it is what God wants for you both too. Enjoy Jaxie's story.

How Dance Helped Me Overcome SM

By Jaxie Russell

When I was four years old I was diagnosed with Selective Mutism. It is an anxiety disorder that made me very shy, nervous, and not want to speak in front of other people. It prevented me from enjoying my life and one of the most important things to me; dance! I loved dancing but my Selective Mutism got in the way. I didn't want to talk or interact with anyone, not even my dance teachers, or my friends. I would purposely hide at the back of the line, hoping I would not be noticed. I just went through the motions, holding back, but secretly wishing I could be more outgoing, like the way I was at home. I wanted to quit so many times but my dance teachers never gave up on me. They were willing to care enough about me, to help me through the rough patch, which lasted many years. This changed my life because they took the time to be patient with me and encourage me at my own pace.

Over time I gained confidence from the encouragement they gave me. I had to overcome a lot. Now I am ten years old and I'm on a dance team at Neisha's Dance and Music Academy that performs and competes in front of large diverse crowds. I go out into the community to perform and interact with people. But I wouldn't be the brave person I am right now, if my dance teachers didn't take the time to care for me. It truly impacted who I am!

Now that I have come out of my shell, I want to impact other people's lives, to show them that I care. My dance studio inspired me, so I have challenged myself to contribute to helping others, especially those who also suffer from Selective Mutism. This year I became a teaching assistant for a group of incredible young dancers at NDMA. Being a teaching assistant gives me the opportunity to help other dancers overcome their fears.

To sum things up, I think it is important to give back to my community so my story can move others. I hope my journey inspires you to go out and make a difference in someone else's life.

Jaxie's story is important to me because she and her friends are my "why" and I work very hard to keep my why in front of me at all times. I know beyond a shadow of a doubt that my own purpose and God-given gifts are to help children find their own why so their inner light will shine brightly. My wish for you is that you will see your own daughter find her God-given gifts so that you can see her light shine. No matter where her journey begins or what her dream destination is, may she follow the map we have laid out in this book to grow into the amazing woman that God created her to be. You can lead her through the journey with the tools that we have discussed. If you find that you need support, pop on over to www.shinegps.com for additional resources. And come back often for the most up to date favorite's list. If you live in the San Diego area or visit our gorgeous city, I invite you to stop into our dance and music school to experience the SHINE movement in full effect; where children are equipped to find their gifts and then joyfully share them with the world. One child at a time; It begins with you and your daughter. Now.

Acknowledgments

I am forever grateful to:

God, for the gifts you have given me to share.

Bernard, for being the strength to all my weaknesses.

My leadership team – Taeko, Ericka, Celia, and Anaid – for carrying the vision.

Misty Lown and MTJGD, for being my Tribe.

To the Morgan James Publishing team: Special thanks to David Hancock, CEO & Founder for believing in me and my message. To my Author Relations Manager, Tiffany Gibson, thanks for making the process seamless and easy. Many more thanks to everyone else, but especially Jim Howard, Bethany Marshall, and Nickcole Watkins.

About the Author

Neisha has dedicated her life to serving children through the arts. Her career spans more than 25 years, including teaching, performing, educating, mentoring, directing, managing, writing, and producing in the dance and music industry. She is the owner and driving  energetic force behind Neisha's Dance & Music Academy in San Diego. As Artistic Director of the Academy, her school has trained and enriched the lives of over 10,000 local children. Neisha is also the Co-Founder and Executive Director of the Chula Vista Ballet Company, a non-profit youth ballet company, serving San Diego's South County. Her most recent enterprise, US Prix de Ballet, is a Ballet Competition and workshop bringing innovation and integrity to the industry.

Neisha is a Charter Member of *More Than Just Great Dancing* and is a Certified Teacher for *Youth Protection Advocates in Dance.* She has served her hometown as a Chula Vista Commissioner for Arts & Culture and was the 2016 Chula Vista Chamber of Commerce Business Woman of the Year! Neisha has been featured in Dance Studio Life Magazine and Success Magazine for her children's programming.

Neisha is a Christian woman and her heart for God and Faith are woven into her message. As a mother to four uniquely-made kiddos, she walks the Motherhood road with you. She shares your joys and struggles! Between her children and her career, Neisha sings and dances her way through life.

Neisha's motto, "Kids are not a distraction from the important work. They ARE the important work." – C.S. Lewis

Thank You

Dear Moms,

My dream is to start the SHINE movement by equipping one million moms across the world to lead their daughters into a life of great love, great service, and great purpose! Thank you for being a part of our SHINE story!

FREE SHINE GPS map: To download your map, visit our companion website. You can also find our companion class and information on our mother/daughter retreat. www.ShineGPS.com.

FREE Strategy Session: Want to talk about how to help your daughter? Get started by filling out the FREE Strategy Session form, which can be found at www.ShineGPS.com

For SHINE support, more information, or to connect with us, email us at info@ShineGPS.com

"When you light someone else's candle, your own candle does not get dimmed. When you light someone else's candle, the whole world gets brighter!"
– MISTY LOWN

Printed in the USA
CPSIA information can be obtained
at www.ICGtesting.com
JSHW080002150824
68134JS00021B/2227